FREE MASK

You Will Need:

- **Thin elastic, wool or string**

- **Scissors**

- **Sticky Tape**

Instructions:

1. Pull out the mask page.
2. Pop out the mask.
3. Cut enough elastic/wool/string to fit around the back of your head.
4. Attach to the back of the mask with some sticky tape.
5. Have fun with your new mask!

SCISSORS ARE SHARP! ASK AN ADULT FOR HELP BEFORE USING.

Contents

Produced under licence by
Pedigree Books Limited, Beech Hill House, Walnut Gardens,
Exeter, Devon EX4 4DH
www.pedigreebooks.com | books@pedigreegroup.co.uk
for

Pedigree®

carte blanche

Tatty Teddy & my Blue Nose friends

Welcome!

We're so excited you're joining us for lots of fun and adventure in our 2014 Annual. We love making friends and playing games... and we can't wait to make friends with you!

Inside our Annual, you'll find loads of brilliant stories, cool quizzes, craft activities, games and even some yummy recipes.

There's so much to discover in our cute blue nose world – step inside and you'll have the best time ever!

When I found out I was going to be in a blue nose Annual, I couldn't stop wagging my tail!

I promised Tatty Teddy I'd be really good, and I wouldn't play any cheeky jokes. See how I got on in the story on page 21.

PS I've left lots of secret pawprints in the pages of this Annual. Find all 20 to unlock a special message!

Write Tatty Puppy's secret message in the pawprints.

E V E R Y O N E

N E E D S   F R I E N D S

Turn the page to start having fun...

Meet Tatty Teddy!

Tatty Teddy was a little brown bear who was once left out in the cold. Snowflakes turned his fur grey and his nose blue.

One night, Tatty Teddy heard giggling coming from the wardrobe. Inside, he found lots of cute new friends

– all with blue noses, just like him!

Tatty Teddy and My Blue Nose Friends live in a fun-filled land where adventure lies behind every magical door.

There are loads of cool places to explore, with laughter and excitement every step of the way!

Tatty Teddy ♥ ♥ ♥ ♥

Giving hugs
Learning to ride his scooter
Reading by his cosy fire

Tatty Teddy can be a shy little bear. But it's hard to stay shy for long when there are so many games and adventures to enjoy in the amazing blue nose lands! Fun and surprises lie behind every magical door, and Tatty Teddy loves exploring with all his special friends.

Tatty Teddy ☹ ☹ ☹ ☹

Falling over
Keeping up with Tatty Puppy

Meet Tatty Puppy!

Tatty Puppy likes to play practical jokes. Once, he tried to turn Tatty Teddy's nose yellow by sprinkling pollen on it!

E

Tatty Puppy is a loveable pup who can't help getting into mischief. But it's impossible to stay cross with Tatty Puppy for long – he looks way too cute with his floppy ears, wagging tail and shiny blue nose!

Tatty Puppy ♥ ♥ ♥ ♥

Eating biscuits
Digging in the garden
Noisy games

Tatty Puppy ☹ ☹ ☹ ☹

Being ignored
Feeling hungry
Sitting still

Walkies Time

Tatty Puppy loves going for walks. Can you colour him in with Tatty Teddy so they are ready to go out together for their walk?

11

Tatty Teddy and the Ex-Stream Adventure!

Tatty Teddy finished his breakfast and looked around his house.

'What shall I do today?' he wondered. 'Perhaps I'll practise riding on my scooter.'

He rubbed his elbow – he'd fallen off last time.

'Hmmm… maybe I'll have a quiet day at home instead,' he decided.

As Tatty Teddy sat by his fire, he couldn't help feeling a little bored.

'I wonder what my blue nose friends are doing?' he thought. That instant, he heard giggling coming from the wardrobe. He opened the wardrobe doors and there was Binky the Panda smiling his big friendly smile.

'Tatty Teddy!' said Binky breathlessly. 'You won't believe what Tatty Puppy has done now. Come through the magical door with me – we need your help!'

Tatty Teddy held his breath with excitement as they stepped through the door. He shut his eyes and wondered which magical land they'd be visiting today…

12

They landed with a soft bump in a grassy clearing. Tatty Teddy blinked as a crowd of cute blue nose friends gathered around him, all talking at once.

'We were playing hide and seek...' said Toots the Elephant.

'...Tatty Puppy hid in the little blue motor car...' said Milkshake the Cow.

'...As usual, he just couldn't sit still...' said Cheddar the Mouse.

'...So he decided to go for a drive...' said Binky.

'And now look!' they all said together.

Tatty Teddy stood up and gasped in surprise. The little blue motor car was stranded in the middle of a fast-flowing stream. Tatty Puppy was standing on top of the car, howling and barking for help.

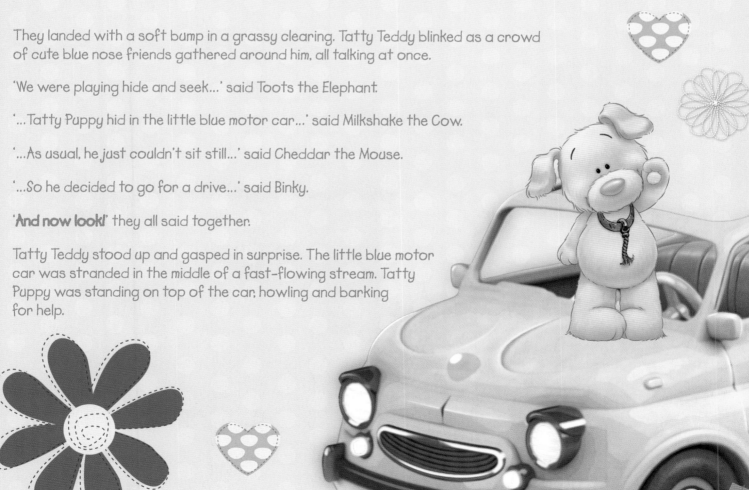

'Tatty Puppy pretends he's good at everything, but the truth is he can't swim very well,' said Binky. 'He tried to drive the car out of the stream, but it keeps getting stuck on the rocks and stones. Tatty Teddy, do you have any bright ideas?'

Tatty Teddy nodded, gave Binky a hug, and set off into the woodland next to the clearing. He didn't have to walk very far before he found the friend he was looking for... Buck the Beaver! Buck was delighted to see Tatty Teddy, and he scampered along with him back to the clearing where the other friends were waiting. As soon as Buck saw Tatty Puppy on top of the stranded car, he understood why Tatty Teddy had come to find him.

In a flash, Buck began to gnaw at a fallen tree on the edge of the woodland. He chewed through the trunk until it was transformed into a huge heap of shredded sticks and bark.

Next, Buck carried some of the sticks into the stream and started to squish them between the uneven stones, piling them up higher and higher. He was building a path across the stream! Tatty Teddy and the friends all set to work too, and soon the path had reached the little car.

Tatty Teddy climbed into the driver's seat and safely steered the car back to the clearing. Tatty Puppy yapped with relief as he bounced off the roof, then jumped up at Tatty Teddy and licked his face all over.

'Sorry for being silly,' barked Tatty Puppy. 'Promise I'll be good for the rest of the day.'

Even though Tatty Puppy had been naughty, Tatty Teddy couldn't resist stroking his cute floppy ears.

'It's nearly time for lunch,' Binky said to Tatty Teddy. 'Peanuts has been baking biscuits, and we have lots of cupcakes too. Can you stay for our picnic?'

Tatty Teddy nodded, just as Milkshake handed him a delicious smoothie.

'My day hasn't been boring after all,' he thought, 'and it looks like there'll be lots more fun to come!'

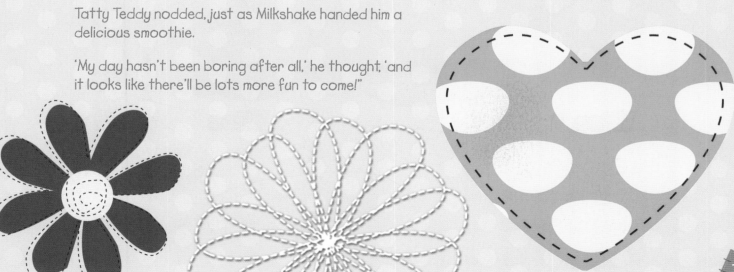

Meet Wise the Owl!

Wise is a fluffy owl who loves to read. But if anyone wants to play, he'll always put his book down and join in the fun.

Reading isn't the only thing that Wise is good at. He's really creative too. He loves painting pictures of his favourite things, especially if his friends join in.

Tatty Teddy and My Blue Nose Friends love playing schools, and Wise is a brilliant teacher! He is always very kind, and hands out lots of gold stars.

Wise ♥ ♥ ♥ ♥

Helping others
Painting
Midnight feasts

Wise ☹ ☹ ☹ ☹

Spelling mistakes
Blunt pencils

Time Wise Time

Wise the Owl is really clever. He thinks a lot, and he can lose track of time completely.

Can you read the clues and draw the hands onto the clock faces?

You need to figure out the correct time from the clues then write in the time in words too.

The time school starts
Clue: Cats are said to have this many lives.

The middle of the day
Clue: It is sometimes called noon, but what number is it?

When I eat my dinner
Clue: this time is the same number as the toes on one foot.

When I go to bed
Clue: This is the same time as the number of days in the week.

It is tricky! But if you can do it Wise the Owl will think you are pretty wise too!

Best Friends Forever!

Tatty Teddy was so happy when he met blue nose friends.
He loves all his friends for different reasons. What about you?

1. Do you have a special friend?
2. What is their name?
3. What colour is their hair?
4. What colour are their eyes?
5. What is your favourite game to do together?
6. Where did you first meet them?
7. How long have you been friends?

E

1. ....
2. ....
3. ....
4. ....
5. ....
6. ....
7. ....

Sketch in Someone Special

Tatty Teddy loves to draw pictures with his friends,

Can you draw your best friend?

Buttoned Together

A friendship bracelet that's fun to make and fun to share.

You Will Need:

- Waxed cotton or good-quality string
- Four-hole buttons, enough to go around your wrist, about 1cm wide
- Masking tape
- PVA Glue

A grown up will need to help you with the measuring and the cutting.

Tatty Teddy loves pretty things, he also loves to make them too. He is making a friendship bracelet for Kittywink. Follow the steps and you can make one too.

1

Cut the waxed cotton or string to a length of about 80cm and fold in half.

2

Tie a single knot in the folded end to form a loop. Before pulling this tight make sure that your loop is the right size for one of the buttons to pass through.

3

Stick the looped end down to the table with some masking tape. Have the two loose ends of cord facing you and thread through two of the holes in the button from behind, with the cord coming out at the front. Cross the cord and thread diagonally through the other two holes in the button from the front to the back and pull tight. Repeat the previous step with as many buttons as you need to go round your wrist.

4

Once you have the correct length, tie a reef knot behind the last button. A reef knot is achieved by passing the right-hand cord over the left and passing it under to knot, then passing the left cord over the right and under to give a second knot.

5

Pull the knot tightly. Put a little PVA glue on the knot. Once this is dry cut the ends and your bracelet is finished. The loop that you made at the beginning will now be used to go over the last button to fasten the bracelet.

Meet Binky the Panda!

Binky is a quiet little panda who likes to daydream. He has a big heart and friends often turn to him if they have a problem.

Binky is a good listener and he's a very loyal friend. If you want to chat about something, he'll always have time to talk.

There's nothing Binky likes more than a game of hide and seek. He's brilliant at hiding in secret places, but he loves finding his friends too!

Binky ♥ ♥ ♥ ♥
Chatting to his friends
Keeping secrets
Exploring

Binky ☹ ☹ ☹ ☹
Hurting anyone's feelings
Shouting
Show-offs

Hidden Friends

Can you find some of Tatty Teddy's blue nose friends hidden in this word search? Tick off each one as you find them.

Z	G	I	G	M	P	U	N	X	E	Q	P	N	Q	E	L
L	P	N	R	H	L	C	E	Y	F	L	A	M	E	T	B
O	M	B	M	L	B	P	E	A	N	U	T	S	E	C	P
P	A	P	I	E	W	L	D	D	R	A	C	N	R	O	V
A	S	D	Y	G	L	P	O	E	U	F	H	N	R	C	I
B	I	F	E	E	W	B	H	S	S	S	L	D	I	O	A
K	A	S	H	N	P	X	I	A	S	N	W	Z	C	E	H
P	H	S	I	D	S	S	E	N	R	O	S	C	Q	A	O
A	S	D	P	O	Y	U	D	J	K	J	M	Y	D	Z	E
I	E	K	L	M	U	M	S	S	G	Y	O	I	N	N	G
U	B	L	G	N	F	G	O	Q	L	T	Y	A	H	Q	T
P	A	F	K	N	G	A	N	B	S	S	E	T	G	A	M
H	C	F	P	A	S	S	O	M	E	C	E	M	P	R	B
F	E	I	O	E	F	N	R	S	E	Q	E	T	S	U	S
T	T	K	G	R	U	S	F	F	F	V	B	C	C	T	T
I	U	F	L	L	L	H	W	W	Q	P	K	G	G	R	D

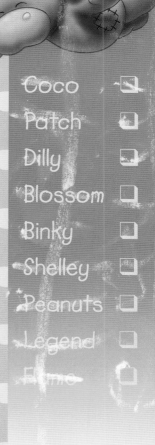

- Coco ☑
- Patch ☐
- Dilly ☐
- Blossom ☐
- Binky ☐
- Shelley ☐
- Peanuts ☐
- Legend ☐
- Flame ☐

Hidden Hearts

Tatty teddy loves hearts, he even has a heart shaped house, but how many hearts are hidden here in his garden?

There is also one very special little friend hidden here too. Who is it?

R

25

Snuggly Sleepover Time!

Tatty Teddy loves having his friends to sleep over. He loves to play and have midnight snacks but most of all he loves being with all his special blue nose friends. So Tatty Teddy has some great tips to make your sleepover a supper snuggly time. Tatty Teddy also loves playing and he has put some of his best games for you to play. See if you enjoy playing them too.

Let's get ready Teddy!

Let your friends know about your sleepover by sending them an invite and make sure everyone arrives in their pyjamas.
You will need to copy the template onto card or ask a grown-up to photocopy it.

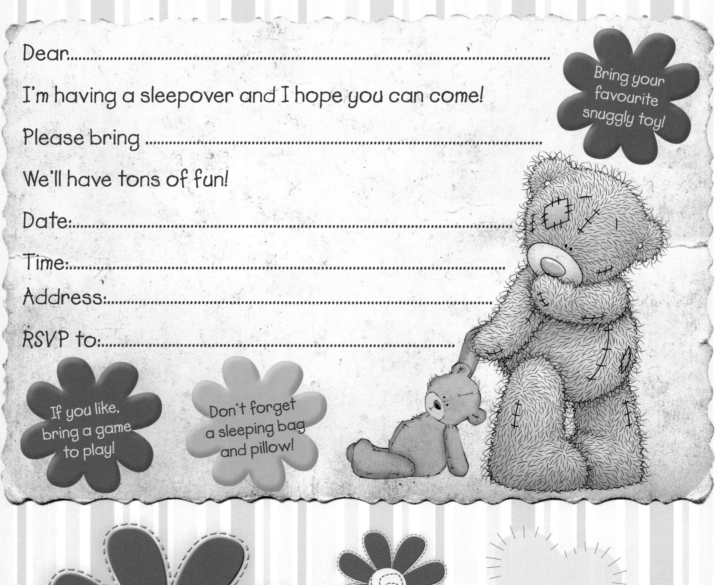

Dear...

I'm having a sleepover and I hope you can come!

Please bring ....

We'll have tons of fun!

Date:..

Time:..

Address:..

RSVP to:..

Bring your favourite snuggly toy!

If you like, bring a game to play!

Don't forget a sleeping bag and pillow!

Hot Chocolate!

Once the sun goes down and you are starting to get a little sleepy, you may fancy a little something yummy and warm for your tummy.
Tatty Teddy loves chocolate. Try making his Hot Chocolate recipe. It's delicious!

Here's what you need:

1700ml of semi-skimmed or whole milk.

280g of chocolate. (Dark chocolate will make your hot chocolate even more tasty and strong).

Marshmallows

Squirty cream

Here's what you do:

1. Gently heat the milk in a pan.

Do not let it get hot enough to boil. (someone will need to watch the milk to make sure this doesn't happen).

2. While the milk is heating break the chocolate into small pieces or you could use a grater to grate it.

3. Once you have the chocolate in small pieces carefully add it to the milk and stir it until all the chocolate melts.

4. Once it is ready pour it into six mugs and add the marshmallows (get a grown up to help again).

5. You could add some squirty cream too just to make it extra yummy!

Sleepover Games

Why don't you and your friends have some fun with these games that Tatty Teddy has suggested. They are sure to make you laugh!

Snuggle Bug

Choose a "Snuggle Bug" by putting slips of paper into a bowl (all blank except for the one that has the SB on it). Whoever picks the "SB" is the "Snuggle Bug". Start the game in the same room (with the lights off throughout the house). The "Snuggle Bug" hides. Everyone else splits up and searches the house calling out "Are you the Snuggle Bug?" If the answer is no, then they keep looking. If the answer is yes, then cuddle up with them in the hiding spot and snuggle up to the SB. As more guests find the SB and snuggle up, the hiding space becomes overcrowded and the game ends when the last person finds the SB. Remember though, no giggling or you will give the game away.

Chocolate Challenge

You need a large woolly hat, a large pair of gloves and a scarf. You also need a dice, a knife and fork, a plate/tray and a bar of chocolate.

The game is so simple, but fun. Everyone sits in a circle and takes turns rolling the dice – if someone rolls a six, they go over to the other side of the room where you've laid out the props. They must put the hat, gloves and scarf on as quickly as possible. Next, dressed in the winter gear, they take the knife and fork and try to cut off one piece of chocolate to eat. They can keep doing this until someone else rolls a six and then the first person up needs to give the next player the hat, scarf and gloves and the second player can try and cut some chocolate off for themselves before another player rolls a six. The game goes on until the chocolate is all gone.

You can modify the rules to suit if you so wish. Perhaps some over-sized gloves will make the job all that bit harder and funnier!

Sleepover Ball Game

Buy a large inflatable beach ball and in permanent marker write questions all over it. Place everyone in a circle and throw the ball to someone. The person who catches the ball must answer the question that their right thumb is touching. After answering the question they then throw the ball to another person. Here are some suggestions for questions:

- What is your favourite colour?
- What three words describe you best?
- Who is your favorite band/singer?
- What is the nicest thing anyone has said to you?
- If you were invisible what would you do?
- If you were an animal what would you be?
- What was your last dream about?
- Who is your favourite My Blue Nose Friend?

One thing you must remember to do on a sleepover – That is sleep! Tatty Teddy always makes sure he gets a good night's sleep!

Party in Progress!

One other thing you may need for your sleepover is...... a Do Not Disturb sign! Trace or photocopy the template of the door hanger onto some card and colour it in. Or ask a grown-up to photocopy it.

DO NOT DISTURB!
Party in progress

y

Meet Blossom the Rabbit!

Blossom the Rabbit loves to have a giggle. She laughs all the time, even while she's doing chores!

Blossom's favourite game is skipping. There's a tree in the woodland garden where she likes to tie one end of her skipping rope. Blossom's friends take it in turns to hold the other end of the rope.

One day, Blossom tried to teach Tatty Teddy how to skip. But Tatty Teddy couldn't get the hang of it, so now he prefers to count Blossom's jumps, to see if she can make it to one hundred!

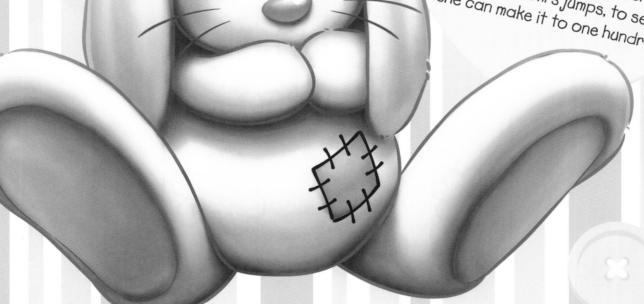

Blossom ♥ ♥ ♥ ♥

Skipping
Doing the laundry
Blowing bubbles

Blossom ☹ ☹ ☹ ☹

Rainy days
Sad faces

Blossom's Garden Challenge

Can you complete Blossom's puzzle? Use the clues to complete the grid below.

5. CARROTS

ACROSS
2. Blossom loves this sweet purple vegetable.
5. Blossom loves these orange vegetables.
6. This vegetable loves to climb.

DOWN
1. This sweet red fruit goes great with cream.
3. Round, red and full of goodness.
4. This vegetable can be mashed, boiled, fried or steamed.

Tatty Teddy and the Blue Nose Beach Party

It was a hot day and Tatty Teddy and My Blue Nose Friends were relaxing at the beach.

'This is the life,' said Scuba the Dolphin, bobbing in the gentle waves.

'So peaceful,' said Ocean the Turtle, sipping an ice-cold drink from the beach café.

Tatty Teddy sunk into a deckchair, shut his eyes and began to drift off to sleep.

CRASH! SQUEAK! BONG!!!

The friends all jumped in surprise when they heard the sound of drums and squeaky pipes coming from the palm trees beyond the sand dunes. Then, hurtling towards them, came what looked like a cloud of flying sand. As the cloud came closer, they realised it was Coco the Monkey. His long tail was swinging wildly and his blue nose shone with excitement.

Coco skidded to a halt just in front of Ocean's deckchair.

'I'm starting a band with Tatty Puppy!' he panted. 'We're having a concert at teatime. Don't be late.'

'That sounds like fun,' said Ocean, brushing the sand from her shell. 'What kind of music are you going to play?'

But Coco didn't answer. He had already scurried off towards the sand dunes, leaving the other friends laughing and shaking their heads. Coco was always so excited – he acted as if every day was his birthday! The friends tried to relax before the concert. But it was impossible with the deafening racket created by Coco and Tatty Puppy.

Clang! Crash!! Shake!!!

It wasn't like any music the friends had ever heard before. Eventually the noise stopped, but it was replaced by the sound of barking and angry chattering.

'Oh dear,' said Ocean. 'It sounds as if Tatty Puppy and Coco are having an argument. We'd better go and see what the problem is.'

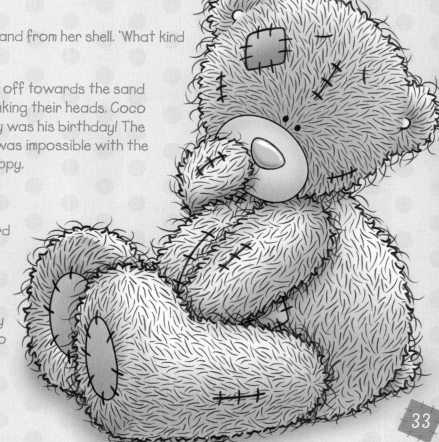

When the friends reached the palm trees, they found Tatty Puppy chasing around the different instruments in a frenzy. He bashed the bongos with his tail and the steel drums with his paws. Then he leapt onto the xylophone and scampered up and down the bars.

'Tatty Puppy just won't listen to my advice,' said Coco, his sticky-out ears waggling in exasperation.

'He wants to play every single instrument, and if he had his way, he'd play them all at the same time!'

Tatty Teddy was very good at calming down his friends when they were feeling upset. He gave Coco a hug while Scuba called Tatty Puppy over and told him in a very stern voice:

'Sit!' Tatty Puppy crept towards Scuba and sat down in the sand looking guilty.

'If you want to be in Coco's band, you'll have to learn how to share,' said Scuba.

Tatty Puppy whimpered and swished his tail. Coco looked around at his friends and suddenly smiled.

'I know,' said Coco. 'Why don't we all play an instrument each?'

Tatty Teddy felt a little worried. He wasn't sure whether he was a very musical bear.

'Tatty Teddy, you'd be brilliant with the pan pipes. They're soft and gentle, just like you!' said Coco. 'Scuba can take the harp and Ocean the steel drums. I'll stick with the bongos and Tatty Puppy can have the xylophone.'

The friends rehearsed together for the rest of the afternoon. Coco gave them all some great tips and before long they were note-perfect (well... almost).

Passion the Love Bug fluttered past. When she heard the cool music, she flew all around the blue nose lands telling everyone about the concert. By teatime a cheering blue nose crowd had gathered to hear Coco's beach band. Everyone danced and drank pineapple smoothies. They had a brilliant evening, and Tatty Teddy discovered he was quite a musical bear, after all!

Meet Paws the Persian Cat!

Glamorous and super-fashionable, Paws likes to groom herself to perfection. It's her ambition to become a catwalk queen!

Paws never goes anywhere without her handbag and hairbrush, just in case she gets the call for a top modelling assignment!

Although she spends hours trying to look her best, Paws always has time for her friends. She's kind and caring and never makes catty remarks.

Paws ♥ ♥ ♥ ♥
Pink glittery things
Posh shampoo
Hanging out with friends

Paws ☹ ☹ ☹ ☹
Tangles in her fur
Early nights

Meet Legend the Unicorn!

E

Legend is a magical unicorn who has an amazing memory. He knows hundreds of songs by heart and loves to sing with his friends.

There's only one problem that Legend hasn't been able to solve... how to stop Tatty Puppy from being so naughty!

Legend is brilliant at answering questions and solving problems. He seems to know the answer to everything!

Legend ♥ ♥ ♥ ♥
Learning new songs
Rainbows
Flying with Flame the Dragon

Legend ☹ ☹ ☹ ☹
Thunderstorms
Practical jokes

Binky's Hide and Seek

How about Binky? He really blends in.

Can you see Truffles too?

Where could Konker be hiding?

Tatty Teddy and six of his blue nose friends are playing hide and seek with Binky. They're so good at hiding. Can you find them all.? Look for **Tatty Teddy** first.

E

Where is our unicorn friend, Legend?

I hear a buzz. Could it be Honey?

Finally, can you find Peekaboo?

39

Meet Coco the Monkey!

Coco loves to be the centre of attention. He's so excitable – especially when he gets together with Tatty Puppy!

Every day Coco practises his bongo drums. He can play loads of other instruments, too, like the pan pipes, the double bass and the steel drums.

Coco isn't just a good musician, he's a great dancer too! His favourite place to dance is a sandy beach on a warm summer evening. He's even happier when all his friends join in the fun.

Coco
Sand tickling his toes
Playing music
Pineapple smoothies

Coco
Grumpiness
Sunbathing

Coco's Crazy Cupcakes

Coco and Peanuts have been baking and are now tucking into their delicious creation. Can you spot the difference? There are six to find.

A

B

It's Party Time!

Tatty Teddy loves to have a party with his friends. Here's what he enjoys the most.

Tatty Teddy loves to... eat yummy treats!

Tatty Teddy loves to... sing with friends!

Tatty Teddy loves to... dance all night!

Tatty Teddy loves to... give presents!

WITH LOVE x

P is for Party!

Tatty Teddy is having a party and you and your friends are invited. So, let's get those invitations out!

Copy or ask a grown-up to photocopy this invitation for you so you can invite all your friends.

Dear...

Please come to my party!

It will be Tatty-Teddy-tastic!

It will be on: ....

At: ....

I hope you can come!

Love from: ....

RSVP...

So what kind of party will you be having?

It could be a make-over party:

Ask your friends to bring some sparkly accessories like hair clips and dressing-up jewellery. You could also ask to borrow some make-up from your mum or a big sister. Experiment with different hair styles and make-up to create some cool new looks. For a really funny game, you could even try a blindfolded makeover. Wear a blindfold and try to put lipstick on your friend! Don't attempt to apply eye make-up when blindfolded, though – it could be unsafe.

How about a crazy cupcake party?

You will need some plain fairy cakes, buttercream icing, ice cream cones and some sweets and sauces. An upside-down cone makes a great princess tower that you can then decorate with icing and sweets.

Have you tried Face painting?

Ask a grown-up to buy special face paints – ordinary paints won't work so well, and may irritate your skin. Choose your favourite My Blue Nose Friend and ask your friend to transform you into that character.

Tip: don't forget the blue nose!

It is always great fun to have a theme to your party:

There are so many different themes you could choose from, such as a princess party, a mermaid party or a beach-themed party. How about a magical party – Legend the Unicorn would love that!

Tatty Teddy's Tuck-in Time

As it is party time why don't you have a go at this easy yummy recipe?

Pizza Pinwheels

You will need

- 375g pack ready rolled puff pastry (thawed if frozen)
- 6 tbsp ready made pasta sauce (not too chunky)
- 100g wafer thin ham
- 100g mature cheddar , grated
- 1 egg , beaten
- 1 tsp dried oregano or mixed herbs

Here's what to do

1. Get a grown up to turn on the oven to 200c/gas mark 6 for a conventional oven, or 180c if it is fan assisted.

2. Take the pastry out of the fridge one hour before you need to use it. It is easier to handle if it is room temperature.

Sprinkle the work surface with some flour (you won't need a lot). Roll it out until it is 40cm x32cm.

3. Spread a layer of pasta sauce all over it, but leave a space around the edge of about 1cm. Sprinkle the ham all over the Pizza and then scatter the grated cheese over it.

4. Now for the tricky bit. Ask a grown up to help start you off with the rolling. Working from one of the shorter ends roll the pastry over as tightly as you can. It will make a really long sausage shape. Put it in the fridge for 10 minutes.

5. Once chilled place it on a chopping board. You will now be cutting it, but need a really sharp knife, so ask a grown up to help you again. They will need to cut it into 12 even slices.

6. Place them down flat on a non stick baking sheet. Brush them with the beaten egg and sprinkle over the herbs.

7. Ask a grown up to place them in the oven and bake them for 12-15 minutes. You will know when they are ready as they will be all puffed up and golden. Let them cool for 5-10 minutes and then tuck in!

44

The Fizz Berry

You will need
- 100g blueberries
- 100g blackberries
- 50g raspberries
- 10 ml lemon juice
- 1 teaspoon caster sugar
- Soda water

Here's what to do

1. Put all the berries into a blender with the lemon juice and the sugar. You may need to ask a grown-up to help with this bit.

2. You will need a small sieve. Put the sieve on top of a tall glass. Pour your blended berries into the sieve. This will strain out all the pips and bits (you can leave them in but that will make it more like a smoothie.)

3. Top up the glass with soda water and add some ice and enjoy.

4. The next one is super easy, so you won't even need a grown up to help.

Cranberry Quencher

You will need
- 1 part cranberry juice
- 1 part orange juice
- 2 parts lemonade

Here's what to do

1. Fill a tall glass with ice.

2. Pour in the cranberry and orange juice. Stir well.

3. Top up with lemonade and it's ready. Delicious!

Blossom's Bunting Bonanza

Blossom knows that Tatty Teddy loves his heart shaped house, he also loves daisies.

So, with all her blue nose friends they are getting together to decorate Tatty Teddy's house as a big surprise.

This bunting is going to look wonderful on Tatty Teddy's heart shaped house. Why not make your own for a super-cute party decoration?

You will need

- toilet tissue cardboard tubes
- poster paint in assorted colours
- PVA glue
- coloured string
- rolling pin
- scissors
- clothes pegs
- paintbrush
- newspaper

Here's what to do

1. Press the cardboard tube flat lengthways. Then roll it even flatter using the rolling pin.

2. Cut the tube into six equal sections to make six 'oval' petals.

3. Put the first ring flat and lengthways on your work surface and put on some PVA 1.5cm in from one folded edge. Put a second ring so it is lying flush with the ring below. Repeat this process for all six rings and then hold the stack together with the peg. Let it dry.

4. Fan out the daisy and glue together the last two rings.

5. Make as many daisies as you can then paint them all. Make sure you use some newspaper so you don't get too messy with the paint.

6. Once they are dry thread them onto ribbon or string, to make a beautiful daisy chain.

D

Meet Passion the Lovebug!

Passion enjoys growing flowers in her garden, but she also loves to flutter around all the exciting blue nose lands. You never know where she'll appear next!

Passion would never hurt anybody's feelings. She's quite a chatterbox, but she always thinks carefully before she gives an opinion.

Everyone falls for Passion the instant they meet her! She has such a bubbly, infectious personality.

S

Passion ♥ ♥ ♥ ♥
Giving compliments to friends
Making daisy chains
Sharing surprises

Passion ☹ ☹ ☹ ☹
Raindrops on her wings
Thoughtless remarks

Passion for Cuddles

Passion loves cuddles with her friends, but one of these pictures of Passion is not the same as all the others. Can you spot the odd one out?

F

A

B

C

D

E

F

Let's Go Outside!

The sun is shinning – let's go out and play! Tatty Teddy loves his garden and there's nothing he likes better than having a picnic with his blue nose friends.

Tatty Teddy has been having a good think and has come up with some top tips for a picnic.

• Tatty Teddy knows that the one thing you really need is a lovely soft Picnic blanket to sit on. A picnic is not a picnic without one.

• Tatty Teddy loves to pack lots of yummy food, you could too.

• How about some sandwiches? You could invite mum and dad to a picnic you have made yourself.

• You could bring some crisps and biscuits too and how about some yummy homemade Lemonade, not the fizzy kind but the old-fashioned kind.

• Don't forget you will need plastic plates and cups.

• If the weather turns a little cold, you could always make the yummy Hot Chocolate from page 27.

Yummy Homemade Lemonade

Here's what to do

1. Ask a grown-up to help you cut the lemons in half and squeeze the juice out of them. If they have a lemon squeezer it'll be easier and also fun.

2. Pour in your squeezed lemon juice and add the weighed caster sugar. Stir the lemon and sugar together with a large wooden spoon.

3. When the sugar starts to dissolve carefully pour in the water a little at a time. Stir the lemonade each time you add more water. You are trying to dissolve all the sugar. Once it is all mixed together you can drink it.

4. Try adding some raspberry juice to make your lemonade turn pink. Pick about six raspberries and then add them in.

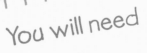

You will need

• 4 lemons
• 1 litre water
• A big jug
• 100g Caster sugar
• A jug that holds about 2 litres.

Pack a Picnic

So what are you going to pack into your picnic, Tatty Teddy has a list of what he is taking, but somehow all the letters have got scrambled, can you help him to unscramble his picnic.?

wdichnas

_ _ _ _ _ _ _ _ _

lppea

_ _ _ _ _

onlemade

_ _ _ _ _ _ _ _

kecpuac

_ _ _ _ _ _ _

elonmrteaw

_ _ _ _ _ _ _ _ _ _

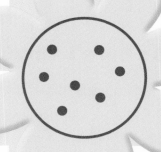

kiooec

_ _ _ _ _ _

51

Let's Go Out and Play!

Here are some of Tatty Teddy's favourite games he likes to play outside with his blue nose friends. If the weather turns bad there's still lots of fun to be had indoors.

Ready Teddy Go!

One person is the traffic light standing away from the other players with their back to them. The traffic light calls "Green light!" while the group tries to get as close to the traffic light as possible. The traffic light turns around quickly, calling "Red light!" and if anyone is spotted moving they have to go back to the starting place. The first person to tag the traffic light wins and gets to be the next traffic light.

Wacky Whispers

This game will get you and your friends laughing, so if you're in the mood for silliness give it a go. Players sit in a circle. One person whispers a sentence or phrase to the next person who repeats it to the person on their other side. This continues around the circle. When it reaches the last person they say the sentence out loud. Will it be correct or something totally silly?

You will need

- Clear container • Rubber band
- Netting or waxed paper
- Spoon • Overripe banana
- Brown sugar • Magnifying glass

Bug detective - Here's what to do:

1. A good way to attract bugs is to put out something sweet like a banana with brown sugar sprinkled on top.

2. Let the banana mixture sit outside a while, then spread it onto the bark of a tree.

3. Check it regularly to see what new bugs you have attracted.

Hole in My Bucket

In the garden, fill a large container with water and place two smaller empty containers about 40 feet away. Split into two teams and give each team an empty milk carton with 10 to 12 holes in the bottom. When you say "go," the first player from each team fills their carton with water, places it on their head and runs to their team's empty container. He or she empties the water into the container then runs back, passing the carton to the next player. The first team to fill its container with water wins the game.

Scavenger Hunt

The idea of a scavenger hunt is to find all items on a list and return them to a designated place as quickly as possible. There are many hunts you could do. Play as individuals or teams, indoors or outside. Here are a few ideas:

- Garden hunt - find things like a red leaf, a stick, a stone, a feather, etc.
- Alphabet hunt – find something for each letter of the alphabet.
- Indoor hunt - find things and tick them off your list without picking them up.

4. Look through the magnifying glass and draw what you see.

5. With a grown-up go out at night with a torch to see if there are any newcomers.

6. If you want to watch a particular bug, put it in your container with a bottle cap of water, a stick, and some green leaves.

7. Cover the container with netting or waxed paper with small holes.

8. Put your bug back where you found it within twenty-four hours.

Sunny Sunflowers

On a sunny day Tatty Teddy loves to spend time in the garden.
Why don't you make a pretty flower pot and plant a sunflower?
It will probably grow to be even taller than you. Wow!

Here's what to do

1. Now you are ready to paint your pot. Look around the garden for ideas. Will you decorate your pot with a pretty painted flower? A bright fluttery butterfly? Or a buzzing bee.

2. Paint your picture onto the flower pot and let it dry.

3. Fill the pot to the top with compost. Make a hole with your finger in the middle of the compost about 3cm deep. Put your sunflower seed into the hole and lightly cover it with soil.

4. Place it in a warm and sunny place and then water it. Wait for it to sprout and then see just how tall it will grow! Remember not to let the soil dry out.

Home Is Where The Heart Is

Tatty Teddy has a cosy home where he loves to spend time with his friends. He loves his heart shaped house.

Have a go at colouring in his house using the numbered colours to help.

1

2

3

4

5

1

1

3

4

4

5

2

57

Meet Cottonsocks the Sheep!

Cottonsocks is the snuggliest sheep you can imagine! She loves cuddling up with her friends.

On cold nights, Cottonsocks stays indoors and plays card games with Tatty Teddy in front of his cosy fire.

Cottonsocks has a secret talent – she's brilliant at knitting. If one of her friends wants a new scarf, she'll knit one in no time!

Cottonsocks ♥ ♥ ♥ ♥
Cuddles
Card games
Hot chocolate

Cottonsocks ☹ ☹ ☹ ☹
Running races
Dropping stitches

Fill in The Fluff!

Can you connect the dots to see who is so soft and fluffy that their fleece is tickling Passion the Lovebug? Once you discover who it is finish the picture by colouring it in.

E

Passion's Colour Crisis

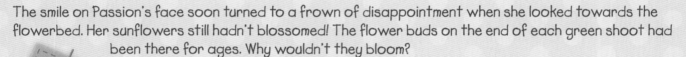

Passion the Lovebug was excited.

'Perhaps today is the day!' she said to herself, as she fluttered down towards the woodland garden.

Her beautiful sparkly wings shimmered in the sunlight as she landed near the garden pond.

The smile on Passion's face soon turned to a frown of disappointment when she looked towards the flowerbed. Her sunflowers still hadn't blossomed! The flower buds on the end of each green shoot had been there for ages. Why wouldn't they bloom?

'I planted them in a sunny spot,' thought Passion. 'And I've watered them every day. I just can't understand it.'

Passion decided to visit her friend Buck the Beaver.

'Buck is brilliant at gardening,' she thought. 'He might know the answer.'

Passion found Buck in the stream, practising his underwater somersaults. He swam onto the bank, shook his fur and gave Passion a hug.

'Of course I'll come to the garden with you,' said Buck. 'I don't know if I'll be able to help, but I'll try my best.'

When the two friends reached the garden, there was a surprise in store. The buds had finally opened out, but the flowers weren't yellow. They weren't red either. Or orange. In fact... they weren't any colour at all!

'That's odd,' said Buck. 'I've never known a see-through flower before. It's quite cool!'

'I don't think it's cool,' said Passion. 'I think it's weird. I planted yellow sunflowers because they're so bright and cheerful. These aren't yellow, they're just... nothing!'

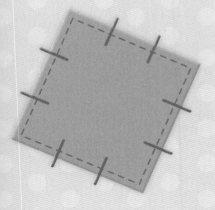

Buck couldn't bear to see Passion upset. He put his arm around her and wished he could do more to help. Just as Passion started to feel a little better, it began to rain.

'Oh no!' said Passion. 'I hate it when my wings get damp. This isn't turning out to be a very good day at all.'

Buck looked up and noticed something shining through the clouds.

'Look, Passion,' he said. 'A rainbow!'

They both gazed at the sky. The rainbow seemed to be streaming down towards them, right into the flowerbed. Something else was coming towards them, too. It was their friend, Legend the Unicorn! Magical stardust sprinkled from Legend's fur as she landed in the garden.

'Flap your wings, Passion!' Legend. 'The stardust will fly through the air and land on the petals.'

Passion flapped as hard as she could, and the sparkly stardust spread all around the garden. When it landed on the sunflowers, the petals suddenly transformed. They weren't see-through any more – they were all the colours of the rainbow!

'Legend, you're amazing!' said Buck. 'Our garden has never looked so colourful.'

Passion hugged Legend then fluttered high into the air.

'I think we should celebrate with a garden party,' she said. 'I'll go and invite all our friends.'

'Brilliant idea!' said Legend. 'Everyone can wear their favourite colours. Red, yellow, purple, pink and not forgetting...'

'**BLUE** noses!' they all laughed together.

63

Meet Truffles the Pig!

If you're saving a bar of chocolate, watch out! Truffles finds it very hard to resist treats, even when they don't belong to him.

Although he can be greedy, Truffles tries hard to be kind and generous to his friends. His hero is Tatty Teddy, because he knows that Tatty Teddy always puts others first.

Truffles' favourite hobby, apart from eating, is taking photographs. He has lots of photo albums, filled with pictures of his most memorable meals.

Truffles ♥ ♥ ♥ ♥
Treating his friends
Extra-large scoops of ice cream
Feeling full

Truffles ☹ ☹ ☹ ☹
Small portions
Skipping games

64

Truffles' Yummy Ice Cream Lollipops

Truffles wants to make a tasty treat for his blue nose friends. You could make some for your friends too.

You will need

- A tub of ice cream – any flavour you like (1 litre size)
- Some cocktail sticks
- 2 x 200 gram bars good quality chocolate (milk or dark).
- Greaseproof paper or non-stick baking paper

These tasty treats are easy to make but need a little time to set so make sure you make them early enough. They can keep in the freezer once made and are so yummy!

Here's what to do

Firstly as you are working with ice cream, you have to work quite quickly so getting everything ready and in order helps.

1. Cover two freezer safe plates with the non stick baking paper. Put one into the freezer.

2. Ask a grown-up to help you with the next bits. Ask them to cut off both ends of the cocktail sticks, leaving them blunt.

3. Get out your ice cream and using a small scoop make small balls of ice cream (if you have no scoop you can use two tea spoons to shape them). Place them onto your chilled plate and push a cocktail stick into them, so it is sticking out of the top. Chill them for 2 hours until solid.

4. Ask a grown up to fill one third of a pan with hot water. Next, break up the chocolate and place it into a glass bowl (the bowl needs to fit onto the top of the pan with the hot water).

5. Ask a grown-up to put the pan on and once the water is simmering place the bowl on top of the pan. Let the chocolate melt, mixing it with a wooden spoon. Once it's all melted take the pan off the heat.

6. Take your ice cream lollipops out of the fridge. Carefully holding the stick, coat each one with the melted chocolate.

7. Have bowls of sprinkles to tip them into.

8. Once decorated stand them on the greaseproof baking sheet and pop them back into the freezer.

65

A-Z of Blue Nose Friends

A is for Alaska
The confident husky who loves to take charge... stick behind her and she'll always lead you down the right track.

B is for Baffle
The sly fox who will amaze you with his tricks... watch closely, otherwise he might puzzle you even more.

C is for Cheddar
The sensible field mouse who is mature about things... she'll never shy away from a slice of the fun!

D is for Dilly
The fluffy duck who's sure to raise a smile... and keep you chirpy

E is for Echo
The playful little bat who loves to stay up late... he'll hang around with you all night long!

F is for Float
The chilled-out manatee who loves to spend half his day sleeping... mess up his routine and he'll be all at sea.

G is for Gumgum
The gentle koala who can sleep anywhere... but he's happiest tucked up with you.

H is for Honey
The daydreaming bumble bee who floats about all day... and will always stick by your side!

I is for Ivory
The no-nonsense rhino who gets straight to the point.. lock horns with her and you'll soon know who's in charge.

There are so many My Blue Nose Friends to love! Do you have a favourite?
Read Tatty Teddy's A-Z below to learn all about them.

J is for
Jock

The strong moose with a tender heart... he's someone you can always lean on.

K is for
Koodoo

The dynamic antelope who loves to rise to a challenge... she's leaps and bounds above all other antelopes.

L is for
Lily

The delightful little frog who hops from place to place... but will always be happy to share your pad!

M is for
Mack

The laid-back otter who loves to float around... with you as a friend, he won't drift far.

N is for
Needles

The hilarious woolly mammoth whose jokes will have you in stitches... stay cottoned on and you'll have a ball!

O is for Oasis

The honest camel who would never take you for a ride... stay truthful to her and she won't get the hump.

P is for Peekaboo

The clumsy mole who always seems to be getting lost... though she'd swear blind that it's never her fault!

Q is for Quiver

The daring Emperor Penguin who loves to skate on thin ice... on the flip side there's no chance of your friendship cracking.

R is for Rocky

The heroic lion... your fearless friend who will always look after you.

S is for Sugarcube

The helpful little donkey... he'll carry you through life when you need him.

T is for Thomas

The huggable hippo who likes to sleep... snuggled up next to you!

U is for you

My Blue Nose Friends want to be friends with U!. Stick a picture of yourself in the white space.

V is for very cute

My Blue Nose Friends are totally unique and very special. Use this space to create your own new blue nose friend for Tatty Teddy.

W is for Whiskers

The smooth-talking seal who'll never get you caught up in anything fishy!

X is for eXtra

As in extra cute just like all the Blue Nose Friends!

Y is for Yabber

The chattering duck-billed platypus who has the gift of the gab... whatever the situation, he'll talk his way out of it.

Z is for Zee Zee

The stubborn goat who never gives in... but he would never lock horns with you!

D

Meet Peanuts the Hamster!

There's always a delicious smell drifting from Peanuts' kitchen. He likes to make sure his store cupboard is full of healthy snacks... and plenty of yummy biscuits, too.

Peanuts is a creative little hamster. He enjoys decorating the biscuits he makes, and loves to add a personal touch especially for his friends.

Peanuts is sleepy during the day and busy at night. That's why there's often a light shining in his house if you pass by when it's dark.

Peanuts ♥ ♥ ♥ ♥

His collection of cookie cutters
Bake-offs with friends
Counting stars

Peanuts ☹ ☹ ☹ ☹

Arguments
Anyone who doesn't share

Peanuts' Amazing Maze

Peanuts loves to play. He is also really clever but this time he is a little stuck. Can you help him find his way through the maze to play with Tatty?

Start

Finish

71

Who Knows Tatty Teddy Best?

Answer all these questions below to prove that YOU do!
Circle the one that you think is correct.

1. Tatty Teddy is:
confident
TRUE or FALSE

2. Tatty Teddy can be:
clumsy
TRUE or FALSE

3. Tatty Teddy is:
shy
TRUE or FALSE

4. Tatty Teddy is:
loud

TRUE or FALSE

5. Tatty Teddy is:
thoughtful

TRUE or FALSE

6. Tatty Teddy is:
quiet

TRUE or FALSE

S

Let's Race, Scoot!

Scoot is ready to rush off, so draw him quickly before he scoots!
Copy the detail from each square in the grid below into the empty grid on the opposite page.

Farewell, Friends!

We've had so much fun together, but now it's time to say farewell...
Here's how to say goodbye in many different languages:

In Spanish we say;
"Adios"
This means "Goodbye"
Say it like this; ah-THYOHS

In Italian we say;
"Arrivederci"
This means; "Goodbye"
Say it like this;
ahr-REE-va-DER-chee

In French we say;
"À bientôt"
This means "See you soon"
Say it like this; ah-bee-EN-toe

In German we say;
"Tschau"
This means; "Bye"
Say it like this; CHOW

In China we say;
"Joy-gin"
This means "Goodbye"
Say it like this; joy-G-in

Answers

Page 7
Tatty Puppy's Secret message is:
EVERYONE NEEDS FRIENDS

Page 17 – Time Wise Time
Time school starts: 9 o'clock
Middle of the day: 12 o'clock
When I eat my dinner: 5 o'clock
When I go to bed: 7 o'clock

Page 23 – Hidden Friends

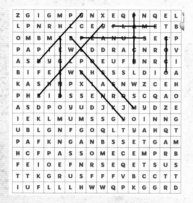

Page 24 – Hidden Hearts

Passion is hiding in the sunflowers

Page 31 – Blossom's Garden Challenge

Page 39 – Binky's Hide and Seek
Tatty is behind the flowers.
Binky is behind the tree.
Truffles is behind the bush.
Konker is at the top of the slide.
Legend is on the roof of the Schoolhouse.
Buzz is behind the treehouse.

Page 41 – Coco's Crazy Cupcakes
1. Peanuts' patch has changed colour
2. There's a bit more icing on Coco's tail
3. One of the heart sprinkles has changed colour
4. The cupcake case has changed colour
5. One of Coco's eyebrows is missing
6. Peanuts' tail is missing

Page 49 – Passion for Cuddles
C is the odd one out
– A heart is missing from Passion's wings

Page 51 – Pack a Picnic
SANDWICH, APPLE, LEMONADE,
CUPCAKE, WATERMELON, COOKIE

Page 71 – Peanuts' Amazing Maze

Page 72 – Who knows Tatty Teddy Best?
1. False
2. True
3. True
4. False
5. True
6. True

Tatty Teddy & My Blue Nose Friends Annual 2014

Visit **Pedigreebooks.com** to find out more on this year's **Tatty Teddy & My Blue Nose Friends Annual,** scan with your mobile device to learn more.

Pedigree Books, Beech Hill House, Walnut Gardens, Exeter EX4 4DH